THE
ENGLISH AT TABLE

JOHN HAMPSON

*WITH
8 PLATES IN COLOUR
AND
25 ILLUSTRATIONS IN
BLACK & WHITE*

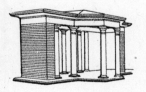

WILLIAM COLLINS OF LONDON
MCMXXXXIV

PRODUCED BY
ADPRINT LIMITED LONDON

PRINTED IN GREAT BRITAIN BY
CLARKE & SHERWELL LTD NORTHAMPTON
ON MELLOTEX BOOK PAPER MADE BY
TULLIS RUSSELL & CO LTD MARKINCH SCOTLAND

LIST OF ILLUSTRATIONS

PLATES IN COLOUR

BLACK AND WHITE ILLUSTRATIONS

THE GLUTTON
Drawing by Thomas Patch
1725-1782

PREAMBLE

ENGLAND'S food has been recognised for centuries, and by all sorts and conditions of men, as excellent ; on the other hand her cooks have won but little renown. Why, if the food is so good, is the cooking so often mediocre ? Perhaps there is an answer to the paradox. Are we not famous for certain dishes, for Roast Beef, for Porterhouse Steaks, for Bacon and Eggs and Apple Pies ? Always (one must make a proviso here), providing the cook *can* cook, where can better examples of our national fare be found than at home ? We have other dishes too, less widely known but not less delicious—a short list must include such items as devilled bones, silverside of beef, saddle of mutton, pork-pies, fried whitebait, fried Dover sole, oyster patties, grouse, oxtail soup. Then there are the pies and the puddings, the cakes and the biscuits. Have we not given the world the pudding and the savoury ? And do we not proffer, with equal, if mistaken generosity, custard sauce on the one and bottled sauce on the other ? But with all our virtues and our vices in the matter of food, we have, from the earliest times, been noted for our hospitality. We have always enjoyed feasting ; an inheritance from our Celtic ancestors : great events and small events, all need their celebration, how better than by the preparation and the sharing of a meal. In the past we have been a fortunate race, living in a land of historic plenty. The English have always liked plain food ; the one qualification was that there had to be plenty

7

of everything. Our climate may explain our tastes to some extent, and if Brillat-Savarin is right when he tells us: "The destiny of nations depends upon the manner in which they eat," the compliment is rather to our appetites than our cooks. To quote again from *Physiologie du Gout* : "Tell me what you eat and I will tell you what you are" is a dictum, which would flatter few of us as individuals. Our climate has provided us with excellent appetites, our great plenty has made us extravagant ; our fine quality has made us careless. But when, as sometimes happens, we take the necessary trouble over the preparation of our simple fare, we can, within limits, do excellently. Certain of our dishes have achieved world fame. However badly we may appear as a nation of cooks, we have always had an astonishing, nay—a passionate, interest in culinary affairs. Let anyone who doubts this statement visit the reference room of any municipal library and inspect the catalogue under the heading of "Cookery," and he will get a very great surprise. Don't think it began with good Mrs. Beeton ! The range goes back long before her time, offering us riches which would have made her blink. And we have not only written these books for the better preparation of good food, but we have bought them and still do, to this very day. Is there a writer in the great bounty of our literature, from Chaucer to Virginia Woolf, who has not paid grateful and graceful tribute to good food (much of it cooked by English cooks) in delicious passages about delicious dishes ? Yet what foreigner dining at one of our modern eating palaces would suppose that the English either cared or knew anything about the art of cooking ? But then English fare at its best is seldom eaten outside a private house : the food served at the average hotel is scarcely likely to win us laurels abroad ; where it is often thought we rely entirely on large pots of boiling water and overhot ovens ! And the sneer (was it of M. Voltaire ?)—"The English have a hundred religions, but only one sauce" is still largely merited by those who cater for our public tables. And yet a famous English eater in the century of famous eating, which makes him a contemporary of the more famous Frenchman, lists more than a dozen different sauces. To put in a good word for that sticky concoction of milk and flour, which steals all too often the respectable title of "melted-butter," would be giving credit where none is due: and yet have we not given the world sauces of our own ? Few to be sure, but all of them good : the sharp red-currant—the astonishing apple—the piquant mint—and the delicious bread-sauce. Are we not the world's prize breakfast eaters, and the "high-tea" is ours, too. Then there are our regional dishes, many of them excellent and far too numerous to be listed here; for every county has its own. Rum butter, pork-pies, potted lampreys, mutton-hams, oyster loaves, lamb's tail pie, junket, damson-cheese, Stilton and Wensleydale. Think of the excellence of farm-house fare ! And so, in spite of watery fish and dripping vegetables, there is a hope for us, in the future perhaps, since the lean years of war have

A FEAST

Detail from the Bayeux Tapestry, late 11th century

A MUSICAL PARTY

done much to make us food conscious. We may have an excuse for our badly cooked vegetables, since it is only a little while ago that we began to use them. Two simple rules would make all the difference, first to buy our vegetables, especially the green ones, daily, instead of once a week, and secondly to abandon the practise of boiling them. Steaming is better in every way, on every count, nor need one fear to be thought un-English by using butter and a frying pan (this refers to the future) as some of our ancestors did; who being fond of food, thought wine and butter not too extravagant for the preparation of delicious vegetable dishes. We have no excuse for our carelessness over fish, since we have been eating it for centuries. Here again, buying is important; fish usually needs care in preparation and cooking, if we prefer good food to indifferent.

The English (if our literature is to be trusted) have known good food when they ate it always; they have complained too, when it was bad. And may they continue to do so until the age old reproach is no longer merited, (here is an Englishman's version) : "God may sende a man good meate, but the deuyll maye sende an euyll coke to dystrue it."

A BUTCHER'S SHOP IN 1798
Coloured engraving published by S. W. Fores

I

The diet of our ancients was, by all accounts, rough and ready ; though according to some authorities, not so simple. Their neighbours, the Gauls, told horrid stories of them and their feasts ; suggesting that human flesh was the meat most fancied on such occasions. The Druids, it seems, were stern food controllers, prohibiting such good things as poultry and hares ; in some parts of the country the use of fish for human food was forbidden, too. They ate twice each day, the second meal being the most important. They drank mead made from the honey of wild bees. They ate what animals they could catch, and wild fruit ; and probably made rough messes of cooked grain.

By the process and progress of trade their succulent oysters arrived in Rome, where such delicacies won the proper appreciation of a race of gourmets. Did this important export lead to the invasion of Britain ? Some historians have believed so, and they may very well be right ; for as history is so apt at repeating, invasions are invariably caused by differences of opinion. The invaders, when they landed in this fertile land, noted the native virtue of hospitality, which has come down to us through the centuries as one of the most pleasing of our national characteristics.

The influence of the Romans on our national diet must have been very considerable. They introduced wine and spice. Their zest for good fare no doubt sent the standard of living soaring for those who were willing to be influenced against the limited ideas of the insular Druids. Soon the Romanised Briton was eating his food off Samian ware, and licking his lips over poultry and fish, which he now, like his conquerors, ate at table. The Romans, it seems, had a poor opinion of trout, but the mullet and the oysters were noble fare. We may forgive, and indeed pity, their failure over trout ; for their influence over the subject-race on the important questions of eating and drinking, was of great benefit to all those willing to consider new, foreign and peculiar ideas. Diet for the new race of Romanised Britons must have been lively and luscious, with the most delicious novelties in the way of eating and drinking. No wonder city life became fashionable under Roman patronage.

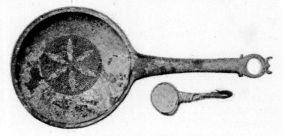

ROMAN KITCHEN UTENSILS

AN EARLY ELEVENTH CENTURY MEAL
DETAIL FROM THE Cotton Ms.

II

But the Romans, having considerably reformed the national diet during their long stay in these fertile islands, returned at last to Rome. The barbarians who followed were bedazed and bedazzled by the richness and plenty they found. They promptly abandoned their fish-eating and sea-faring for flesh foods and farming. The Roman refinements were quickly destroyed, three parts of the country were set aside for the grazing of cattle, sheep, and the growing of grain. Ruthless and hungry, they soon became a race of food producers ; quantity, instead of quality, became the slogan. Their greed led them to grossness, and soon the bulk of the population were busily engaged on the task of keeping supplies up to the demand. Great beef eaters, the Saxons also ate largely the flesh of sheep, and coarse bread. They had a great capacity for drinking, and after the meal had been eaten, the board was carried out, in order to set about the business of toasting each other's healths with copious quantities of mead and ale. They were hospitable. Rich men ate four times a day, at tables furnished with coverings. They used knives, spoons and bowls ; besides drinking horns, they had glass ware of blue, green and amber. In a burial hoard, found in Wiltshire, dating from the latter part of the ninth century, an elaborate, if not too useful, fork was unearthed. The Cotton MS. shows, in one place, three people at a table, served by two kneeling men, presenting prepared food on long spits. The sexes ate together. Their meats were prepared by broiling, baking and boiling ; though generally, if pictorial evidence is anything to go by, their viands were much more lightly cooked than we should find adequate. As part of its rent, a farm of ten hydes paid ten casks of honey, three hundred loaves, twelve casks of strong ale, two oxen, thirty wethers, ten geese, twenty fowls, ten cheeses, one cask of butter, a hundred eels and five salmon. Gardens flourished with the coming of the monks, producing apples, pears, almonds, and even grapes; and, it is said, pears, peaches, chestnuts and mulberries too, which had been first imported by the Romans. Much of the food, especially meat and fish and butter, were heavily salted in order to prevent it going bad. Honey was plentiful and much used in the making of mead. Bread was eaten in the form of small round cakes. Bacon was stored away in little special houses : it is said to have got its name from *bucon*, the ancient name for beech-mast on which the large herds of swine throve. For her food a woman serf was given corn, with a sheep (the Saxons preferred beef) for her winter nourishment, with beans for Lent. In his life of St. Benedict, Ælfric records that the Italians ate oil with their food as the Anglo-Saxons ate butter! The board of Hardecanute was sumptuous in high regal fashion, being prepared four times each day for the whole court. After the feast was finished the scraps and fragments were put out-side for the benefit of those not bidden to the royal table. Fondness for food and drink in those days seems to have made for poor table manners ; though the customs of the Anglo-Saxons were at least more generous and social than those of their Norman supplanters, who noted the good humour, the eagerness to please, the lavish scale of their entertainments, and the fashion in which they gorged and guzzled.

AN EARLY TWELFTH CENTURY MEAL
Illumination from The Gospels
from Bury St. Edmunds Abbey

PREPARING A MEAL
Detail from the Luttrell Psalter c. 1340

III

The Normans were frugal. They brought their own refinements of cooking. They despised the Anglo-Saxon traditions and were in turn despised by the conquered, who considered their frugality merely an excuse for meanness, and lacking vastly in the good old custom of hospitality. The newcomers busied themselves with the building of houses and castles; the making of vast game preserves which they kept jealously for themselves. They were dainty feeders, eating but twice a day, and giving new names to the cuts from Anglo-Saxon animals, despising the offal which they left for their uncouth vassals. Their culinary efforts were more elaborate, but since they had ambitions for longevity they :

"Rise at five, dine at nine
Sup at five, bed at nine."

From the early chroniclers we learn Norman princes only provided one meal a day at their courts. No wonder the Anglo-Saxons thought such fastidious habits parsimonious. Henry of Huntingdon gives many fascinating details of the early days and ways. It is he who informs us of regional sources : "Winchester for wine, Hereford for herds, Worcester for corn renowned . . . for fishes Canterbury." Wildfowl and game of all kinds

13

abounded ; with vast supplies of fish ; herrings, oysters, eels, mussels and salmon figure in his list. For a reign or so the Normans remained particular, preferring the customs they had brought over with them to those they found here. Both William of Malmesbury and Fitzstephen comment on the drunkenness and gluttony previously prevalent. And so in spite of all the careful ways of their ancestors, the Normans, while they retained much of their native good taste, eventually developed the hearty feeding proper to the English climate ; and less than a hundred years after the Conquest, the Plantagenets brought in a new era of good fare.

The standard of living, even for poor people, was higher in England than on the continent. Country folk ate "white meats" : that is to say the products of the dairy, milk, cheese, and butter, with an occasional chunk of bacon. Now and again they raided the game preserves of the rich, helping themselves to fish from the rivers and stew-ponds of the monasteries. Their bread was made as they needed it, from corn ground in a hand-mill ; they ate while it was still fresh. In the cities the craftsmen fared somewhat better. But these islands had already endured ghastly periods of famine through the failure of harvests and outbreaks of disease among the flocks and herds. A severe winter, with frosts long into the spring, made fish scarce and costly ; such lean periods were inevitably followed by epidemics of plague which slew thousands of people whose health had been reduced by the rigours they had undergone. The monasteries did much to promote husbandry. The Anglo-Saxons had grown apples from which they had made cider. They also had plums ; strawberries and raspberries flourished, but probably in a wild state. They grew pine trees too; pine kernels were much used in dishes during the Middle Ages. Alexander Neckham, who wrote the first cookery book, also gave an account of the English garden. Onions, leeks, cucumbers, lettuces, parsley, mint, sage and many other items were included in his list. It was an age of strong flavours; herbs and spices played an important part in the cooking of the day. The rich wildly tried to grow all kinds of ambitious trees and herbs. They imported olive oil, wine and spices. Neckham gives a whole chapter to the vine-yard ; but if the wine was drinkable, the quantities must have been very small and in no way equal to the large demand. The rich drank spiced wines and cordials, such as hippocras, pigment, morat and mead. William of Malmesbury says that the wine of Gloucester was hardly inferior to that of France. The poor had cider, perry and ale. The boar's head and the peacock were royal dishes, and Kings were rumoured to have died through over-indulgence in their favourite viands. In his treatise on cooking, *De Utensilibus*, Necker gives as necessities of the properly furnished kitchen, a table for chopping and mincing, mortar and pestle, pot-stick, a cauldron, frying pan, vessel for mixing, pepper mill and a contrivance for making bread crumbs.

FEEDING THE CHICKENS
Detail from the Luttrell Psalter c. 1340

Pepper, a most important article in days when strong flavours were the fashion, played a considerable part in the history of our commerce. By the eleventh century there was a guild of pepperers, who later, through their growing importance as importers of sugar and spice, became the grocers. A monk, (a contemporary of Necker's) Jocelin De Brakelond, whose chronicle of his abbey from 1173 to 1202 inspired Carlyle's *Past and Present*, tells us the Abbot had four sorts of dishes on his table, which he maintained with the opulence due to his dignity and position ; though he himself lived simply enough, preferring sweet foods such as milk and honey. But visitors were treated with the ancient hospitality, no stinginess in the matter of meat and drink. He had venison from his own park and fish from his own ponds, which he kept well stocked. King John had a weakness for the lamprey pies which were sent him in tribute each year, receiving the adjective of Royal. The same monarch is supposed to have died from a surfeit of peaches and new cider. Soon the early poet chroniclers were writing of customs and society in feudal England, and we owe much to them for their descriptions of the manners of daily life. Chaucer tells us of the elegant manners of Madame Eglantine, the prioress who :

"Ne wette hir fyngres in hir sauce depe.
Wel koude she carie a morsel, and wel kepe,
That no drope ne fille upon hire breste."

15

And his stout jolly man cook :

> "To boille the chiknes with the marybones,
> And poudre-marchant tart and galyngale ;
> Wel koude he knowe a draughte of Londoun ale ;
> He koude rooste and sethe and boille and frye,
> Maken mortreux and wel bake a pye . . .
> For blankmanger, that made he with the beste."

His Somonour "Wel loved he garlike, onions and lekes." But in spite of Ranulph Higden's description—"Englonde is beauteuous... floure of londes all about that londe is full payed with fruyte," times could be terribly hard on the peasant community as we know from Chaucer and the author of *Piers Plowman*, who tells how in the times of shortage the lord of the manor took away the poor peasant's pigs and geese, his wheats and oats, leaving but a "tally" in receipt. But when times were good the vendors cried their wares in the streets of the towns and cities, and the wealthy sent to London for new and pleasant stores for their cupboards. "Whit wyn of Oseye, and reed wyn of Gascoigne, Of the Ryn and the Rochelle" call the taverners, and the cooks crying "Hot pyes, hot" form part of the Plowman's vision. He instances too the adulterations of knavish vendors who tampered with the quality of the goods they offered for sale. He records the shortage of meat and money ; being unable to afford pullets, geese or pigs. He complains that he has no salt-bacon nor eggs for the making of "Coloppes" (which is evidence of the antiquity of our national breakfast dish). He has, however, some fresh cheese, with loaves made of bean flour and bran, an oat cake, some curds and cream, some leeks and some parsley, and "manye cole plauntes" which seem to have been cabbages from which soup was made. Pottages and mortreux were very popular with all classes of society. The rich made soup from almonds, ginger, and all sorts of novel ingredients, while the poor had to be content with simpler broths, using leeks, onions, beet, cabbage and beans.

The fourteenth century produced the first practical cookery book, *The Forme of Cury*. It was compiled by the Master Cooks of Richard II, a royal gourmet of the first water, if he deserved his reputation as 'Royalist vyander of all Christian Kings,' ; we are told that he entertained ten thousand people daily at his various tables. People seem to have been far more adventurous about food then than we are now-a-days. Their various preserved meats, heavily salted, no doubt demanded the contrast of sharp and pungent flavours ; but cinnamon and ginger sauce with lamb does suggest that palates were much less delicate than are our own.

In his fascinating *History of Domestic Manners* Wright explains the use of *trenchers*, these were loaves of coarse flour and the meat was placed directly on them, so that they served as plates, and the diner first carved

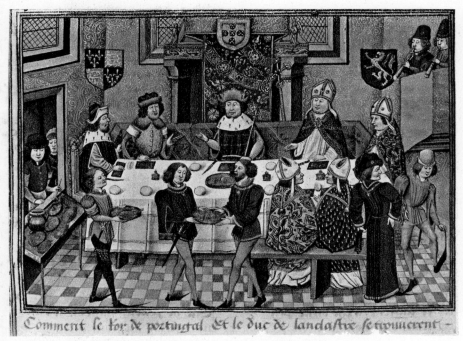

Comment le roy de portugal et le duc de landastre se trouverent-

'THE DUKE OF LANCASTER DINES WITH THE KING OF PORTUGAL'
Detail from an Illuminated Ms., 1387

his portion of flesh and then ate the plate. In later times they went from the tables of the wealthy to the alms basket. Later the trenchers were put on to plates, and soon it was seen that they were anachronisms.

Jack Cade extolled the 'sallet' which he thought created for his good, while Gilbert Kymer was dubious of its propriety, though oddly enough he mentions cabbage, lettuce, spinach and beetroot as being boiled with meat. Vegetables are rarely included in the early MSS., except such as were used in salads. A fourteenth century 'salat' includes parsley, sage, garlic, leeks, borage, mint, peony, fennel and other herbs. The ingredients are to be washed and picked clean ". . . myng him wel with rawe oile, lay on vynegr and salt and sue it forth."

The marriage of Henry IV and Joan of Navarre in 1403 was celebrated by a magnificent feast. Court fare was both sumptuous and bold : flesh of whales, seals and bears figured at such banquets, where three courses of meat were followed by three of fish. Among the latter were sturgeon, turbot, carp, salmon, lamprey, trout, porpoise, perch, also oysters, crabs and lobsters ; while swan, heron, wigeon, crane, bustard, tern, egret, bittern and all the wild variety of 'smal byrdes' helped to make a groaning board. Even the fishy gull was not despised. Each course would be played in on pipes, trumpets and tabours. Mention must be made here of the 'sotelte' which brought each of the six courses to a close. These were elaborate trophies of the confectioner's art, in the nature of symbolic emblems, made of sugar, jelly or paste, constructed with skill, depicting either a legend or a theme which the diners would recognise and appreciate by reason of its familiar or topical nature. At a feast given in honour of John Stafford's elevation to the See of Canterbury in 1443, the first course of eleven dishes was brought to an end by the introduction of St. Andrew, enthroned, with 'bemes of golde,' while small figures of the bishop and his attendant knelt at the saint's feet. This custom, described by Robert May in 1685 as part of the ceremonial for Twelfth Night, was to persist in the establishments of the great as long as "good housekeeping was in fashion among the English nobility" wrote John Nott, once cook to the Duke of Somerset and Ormond, in 1726; which to us now-a-days seems a veritable period of "good housekeeping" on the grand scale.

The *Paston Letters*, written between 1424 and 1506, give many details of the store cupboard needs of that flourishing Norfolk family. Among them figure salt, oranges and herrings. There is also mention of syrup and green ginger of almonds, this sounds delicious but its importance (like that of syrup) was primarily medicinal. In 1471 Dame Margaret sent money to her son in London, instructing him to buy her sugar, dates, and figs ; also demanding the London prices per pound of pepper, cloves, mace, ginger, cinnamon, saffron, almonds, rice and comfits among other items, since she did not wish to purchase in the provinces if these wares could be more cheaply obtained in the Metropolis. Food control is no new thing and dates from ancient times. The sumptuary laws, begun in feudal times, persisted on into the days of Queen Elizabeth. They limited expenditure on food and even ordered a limitation on the number of dishes. Since the main export from this country during the middle ages was wool, we can, I think, take it that mutton figured extensively in the meals of those able to afford meat.

Hospitality was on a prodigious scale. Margery Kemp, author of the oldest known English autobiography, speaks repeatedly of the 'good cheere' pressed upon her, as she went on pilgrimages from one shrine to another : how the Bishop of Lincoln himself sent her 'full kindly' viands from his own table, as she sat at meat among the clerks in his hall. Red herring, 'good' pike and stock-fish are among the dishes offered her. She had been a brewer and then a miller ; but failed at both trades, for it was neither easy to brew good ale or make good flour in those times. Cookery books began to appear in print. In 1500 or thereabouts, Pinson, one of the earliest of English printers, published the *Boke of Cokery*: "Here beginnith a noble boke of festes royalle and Cokery a boke for a pryncis house-

A PAGE ILLUSTRATING A HERBAL
From an Illuminator's Pattern Book, early sixteenth century

holde . . ." Wynkyn de Worde published the renowned *Boke of Kervynge* in 1508, which contained many charming terms for the art of carving as "barbe that lopster," "unlace that coney," "tayme that crabbe," "border that pasty," "spoyle that henne," "dysfygure that pecocke," and many others equally felicitous and descriptive. The carver was instructed not to place more than a thumb and two fingers on the joint. Guests carried their own knives and spoons. They were presented with bowls of water and hand cloths on arriving in the dining hall; the well-bred took care to behave with grace and dignity, or so it would seem, for the instructions given in contemporary writings show how necessary good manners were at table, when meat called for the use of fingers and two people shared the same dish, drank wine from the same cup.

FISHING
Woodcut from Wynkyn de Worde's
edition of the *Boke of St. Albans*

PICTISH CAMP ON THE BANKS OF THE HUMBER
Engraving from Holinshed's *Chronicles of England, Scotlande and Irelande*, 1577

IV

The Tudor period started off badly; civil war had done much to lower the standard of living. Table manners in the houses of the great were bad, the servitors casual, the food indifferent and hospitality ungenerous. The worst and least appetising food was presented first, so that by the time the elegant dishes appeared the guests were satiated. The Earl and Countess of Northumberland had for breakfast on flesh days: bread in the form of trenchers, with two additional loaves of fine meal; their meat, half a chine of mutton or a chine of boiled beef. To wash it down they had a quart of beer and another of wine. The older children got boiled chicken or mutton bones with their bread, with a double allowance of beer, while those in the nursery had similar fare; on fish, or fast-days, they got a dish of butter to their chunks of dry or salted fish, their herrings or sprats. In spite of periodical failures of crops, which led to a vicious rise in the price of grain, and the subsequent horrors of famine and plague, on the whole food was eaten with gusto in good times. By the reign of Henry VIII we had secured for ourselves abroad the title of the world's champion meat eaters. Three reasons given by one of our countrymen while travelling abroad, were our fondness for variety, that the same meat did not suit every stomach; while the third and most ingenious was that this land had such quantities of flesh, fish and fowl, which, if

A TRENCHER BOX
Painted Beechwood.   Early Seventeenth Century

we failed to devour, would rise and consume us. The Tudor regime
brought about great changes in social life, feudalism passed, the monasteries were pillaged and the vineyards abandoned ; but the age found new
riches, and the merchants prospered with the success of commercial
ventures.   Eating conditions altered, meal times too, for the English
were ever given to change in that direction.   At one period two meals
a day were considered sufficient, while at another four were found too few.
The sixteenth century is very fully documented : we travelled abroad
and were visited by people of other races, many of whom left valuable
testimony, since they found our table manners worthy of comment, our
hospitality remarkable, our food and drink excellent.   The printing presses
had heralded a new order ; from this time on, journals, letters, diaries,
books on diet, cooking, and gardening pour forth in an ever-increasing
stream ; the references become far too numerous, the profusion so great,
that only a few selected details can be given and a few sources indicated.
The Venetian Ambassador at the opening of the century thought us great
epicures, but found us mean, since the rich indulged themselves on the
most delicate fare, while their households were fed on coarse bread and
beer and cold meat, 'baked on Sunday' for the week.   He does admit
however that this food was supplied in large quantities.   The English
took pleasure in remaining at table a long time.   They were sparing with
wine, since it was expensive.   Often three or four people shared wine

HENRY VIII
Oil painting. School of Hans Holbein, 1497-1543

from the same cup. The moderate supply of wine was made up by copious quantities of ale and beer.

> "Hops and turkeys, carp and beer,
>   Came in to England all in one year."

is assigned to the early part of the reign of Henry VIII, but it is thought hops were known much earlier.

In 1542 Dr. Andrew Boorde published a book on diet. He had experience of monastic life and had spent much time abroad. He disapproved of water and beer for Englishmen, the latter a new-fangled drink we had learned to brew from the Dutch. Ale and claret he thought excellent, the latter being especially good as an accompaniment to meat. Soup, he suggested, was much used by the English, and very good he considered it. Few vegetables, apart from the onion tribe, win his regard, though he has much to write about herbs. "A good Coke is halfe a physycyon. For the chefe physycke . . . doth come from the Kytchyn." He tells of four sorts of cheese, 'grene,' 'softe,' 'harde' and 'spermyse,' the latter being home-made with curds and the juice of herbs. The 'softe,' being neither too new or old, he considered best.

During the reign of Henry VIII, meals were eaten at eight in the morning, at noon, and again at six, but even as late as this such extra meals as 'an afternoon' or 'after supper' might be called for. Bread,

23

joints of beef and mutton roasted and boiled, with great beakers of ale, characterised these meals. The households of the great were very lavish. Wolsey employed a vast number of men, including two master cooks, a couple for pastry, and two more as bakers. There was a clerk to the spice room, two plate-men, with seven for the cellar.

The Bishop of Nocera thought our variety of food and the quality consumed by a single household in a day 'marvellous.' He found tables spread with 'warm' eatables at every hour of the day. Our 'dense air' he found was our excuse for greediness. But our spokesmen were not silent : the Herald told the French—"Item, for your wyne, we have good ale, bere, metheghelen, sydre, and pirry, beying more holsome beverages for us then your wynes, which maketh your people dronken, also prone and apte to all fylthy pleasures and lustes." By that time the young Edward was on the throne. Wriothesley records a harsh year, when fuel was short by reason of the previous wet summer, how there was a scarcity of Lenten fare, owing to the great cold and protracted frosts, so that fish, salt, dry and fresh, was scarce and expensive; and by Easter, since there had been a cattle plague, meat was in short supply, with lamb and mutton fetching scandalous prices. And the importance of meat in our daily diet can be gauged from William Forrest's assertion "Owre Englische nature cannot lyue by Rooats, by water, herbys, or suche beggerye baggage, that may well serue for vile owtelandische Cooatis ; geeue Englisch men meate after their old vsage, Beiff, Mutton, Veale, to cheare their courage." When Mary of Guise arrived in London the Mayor and Aldermen sent gifts of beef, mutton, veal, pork, sturgeon, quail, wild-fowl, wine, beer, spice and bread. The crowds celebrated Mary Tudor's proclamation with tables in the streets—with 'wine and beer and all.' Matthias Quadt noted the tasty, delicate oyster; while Estienne Perlin heard us 'belch shamelessly at table.' The school-boy got his dinner between eleven and twelve, with supper at five or six, with a breakfast of bread, butter and fruit. The noon meal was often a porridge of wheat or barley, with turnips or cabbage in it, though he might get fish on the appropriate days, fresh if the market prices permitted, if not it would be salt or dry. 'Afternoons' would be bread and fruit, in the summer there would be apples, plums and pears, while in winter there were figs, raisins and almonds. Supper might consist of a joint, boiled or roasted, but perhaps most often a 'fine gallimafrie' or hash, was the main dish. The day-boy, with his pressed grapes and dried figs, was no doubt envied. On fast days, eggs, cheese and nuts eked out the whole-meal bread. Harrison, in writing of the past, refers to 'beverages or nunchions,' and 'rear-suppers.' He thinks life better ordered with only dinner and supper. His details are most vivid and varied. "In number of dishes and change of meat the nobility of England (whose cooks are for the most part musical-headed Frenchmen and strangers) do most exceed, sith there is no day in manner that passeth over their heads

24

SCENE IN A COFFEE HOUSE.

Coloured etching by Thomas Rowlandson, 1756-1827

BILLINGSGATE FISH MARKET

Coloured aquatint by Rowlandson and Pugin

From *The Microcosm of London* Aquatint 1808

wherein they have not only beef, mutton, veal, lamb, kid, pork, cony, capon, pig, or so many of these as the season yieldeth, but also some portion of the red or fallow deer, besides great variety of fish and wild fowl, and thereto sundry other delicates . . . jellies of all colours . . . marchpane . . . conserves of old fruit . . . tarts of divers hues and sundry denominations . . . suckets . . . gingerbread, florentines . . .'' He suggests that more than eighty different kinds of wine were imported and served by the rich merchants at their feasts. Gentle folk had their first meal at eleven, with the second at six. Merchants ate later, and husbandmen later still. The rich had fine silver plate with glass from Venice to set off their fine eating. Queen Elizabeth had a set of China Plates, while Francis Bacon, according to the season, had his table 'strewed with sweete herbes and flowers' at every meal since he found they 'did refresh his spirits and his memore.'

Paul Hentzner, who put down the Queen's black teeth to her fondness for sweetmeats, thought us more polite in eating than the French. We ate less bread and more meat which we 'roste in perfection.' He noted too, how we put a great deal of sugar in our drinks, and considered that the common people looked more healthy than the rich, since they were not able to over indulge in the fashionable weakness for confectionery. Emanuel van Meteren thought we kept too many idle servants, though we fed well and delicately. Lemnius called our meat 'wholsome and exquisite.' In times of prosperity the gay crowds threw oranges and eggs at one another on May Day in London. From the same source we learn, on July 30th, 1557, 'Monser the Machyn de Henry' did, with some friends, eat half a bushel of oysters, by candlelight at eight o'clock in the morning, in an Anchor Lane cellar. The meal included onions, with ales described with prefixes—red, claret, muscatel and malmsey. What a breakfast— and no R in the month either ! He gives many notes on the punishment of black marketeers and dishonest vendors. For hawking pots of straw-berries, packed more than half full of fern, a man was put in the pillory, while another who cheated the fishwives was made to wear a collar of smelts round his neck. A dishonest butcher was paraded round the streets with his face to the horse's tail, with two halves of a lamb slung before and behind, while a raw calf was carried on ahead !

In 1564 'Mr. John Hawkins Esquire' introduced the sweet potato, but more than two centuries had to pass before the 'lazy root' of William Cobbett started on a slow rise to popular favour.

'Fysshe' days were still necessary and an act was passed by Elizabeth ordaining Wednesdays. A proclamation stated that 135,000 head of beef might be saved in a single year 'in the Cittie' by one meatless day each week.

Platter, a visitor from Germany in 1559, saw the preparation and service of a meal to the Queen (though she ate it in the privacy of her own apartments away from the gaze of the curious), portions of meat and bread being transfixed together on the point of the carver's knife. He has great praise for our hospitality, telling of a meal he ate at the Lord Mayor's, who kept open house, entertaining travellers from near and far daily. The courses were all most richly and perfectly prepared, served with delicious sauces, while various dishes lay near the hands of each guest, in order to tempt the appetite. The wines came from France, Greece, Spain and Germany. Our beer he thought comparable in fineness to old Alsatian wine. He thought less of the dessert of sweetmeats, tarts and pastries, for they were not comparable in delicacy to the entrées. He discovered it costly to eat alone in taverns since there was no inclusive charge for a meal.

There were many fulminations against the adulterations of the food and drink purveyors, and many curious remedies for sweetening tainted meat. Greene wrote a vitriolic attack on the nefarious practices of the brewers and vintners. The poor, especially in hard times, mourned the passing of the hospitable monasteries, for while, in a poem, Churchyard sadly recalls the days when the charitable had 'great ioy in spending beefe and bred,' he complains now-a-days that hounds and hawks are fed, while the poor go hungry. Tusser, writing his sound advice in doggerel, advises the countryman to eat his herrings and save the salt fish, since it would be good when Lent was over. Brawn was a good and ever popular dish. He advised the housewife to preside over the carving implements, giving 'a messe' of hot pottage to each with a 'morselle of meate.' He tells of Easter veal and 'bakon,' 'Martilmas beefe'; that 'When Mackrell ceaseth from the seas, John Baptist brings grasse beefe and pease.' 'Michelmas' abounded in fresh herrings and fat sheep, while 'All Saintes doe laie, for pork and souse : for sprats and spurlings for their house.' Butter and cheese had to make up for a lack of fish and fruit.

Matthew Parker, Archbishop of Canterbury, bequeathed, with many another rare volume, *A Proper Newe Booke of Cokerye* to the Cambridge college of which he had been Master. A slim volume of sixteen leaves, it teaches how to make 'a tarte of marygoldes, primroses, or cowslips,' 'to Stew Stekes of Mutton' and 'to make a Whyte Broathe.'

The seventeenth century flashes a starry array of glittering poets and dramatists, rich with epicures and wits ; when lords and ladies wrote cookery books, exchanged recipes for this tart or that cordial. In 1601 Thomas Coryate introduced the fork from Italy, meeting with sneers and quips ; earning the nick-name of 'Furcifer' for his pains. Years elapsed before the fork met with the general response it deserved (though Jonson praised it) ; an elaborate print of Charles I, feasting the Spanish Ambassador, reveals no trace of any such implement.

Shakespeare asked "Doth not the appetite alter ? A man loves meat in his youth that he cannot endure in his age." His numerous references to the food, drink and table manners of his age will be familiar to most

CHARLES II ACCEPTING THE FIRST PINEAPPLE GROWN IN ENGLAND
Engraving by Robert Grave after S. Harding

readers. 'Sherris sack,' which had lost much of its popularity, is the fore-runner of the sherry we know. During the reign of James I, eating houses where one could take an inclusive meal for a stipulated charge became fashionable, and the term of 'ordinary' came into fashion and was to persist well into the nineteenth century. 'Commons,' meals eaten at a college or a common table, were of much greater antiquity.

The pages of contemporary drama are rich in allusions to good living. Dekker offers delicacies as various as 'Biskets,' 'Carowayes,' 'Marmilade,' 'nutmegs' and 'partridge, plover, woodcocks, quailes' and 'Suger-plums and Pippin-Pies, gingerbread and Walnuts.' Feasting in the reign of the first Stuart King was prodigal; his household expenditure amounted to a hundred thousand pounds a year, double the sum spent by Elizabeth. Four huge pigs, bitted and harnessed with reins of sausages to an enormous bag-pudding, figured as the chief dish on one occasion. There was a great variety of wine and much zest in drinking, which a visit of the King of

27

Denmark did much to encourage, since it reintroduced the toast, in all its ancient quantity ; in a company of twenty-five or thirty, each person's health was drunk in rotation ; sometimes a toast was proposed to an absent patron, or a lady, as a proof of love or loyalty. Fynes Moryson gives an impressive picture of the excellence of English inns and tells how a traveller might eat a good meal for sixpence at the landlord's table, adding ". . . English Cookes, in comparison with other nations, are most commended for roasted meates." This Scots traveller also writes of 'Vsquebagh,' a liquor which was the earliest form of whisky. While Thomas Muffet M.P., who died in 1604, left an MS. of some culinary and dietetic importance behind him. In *Health's Improvement*, he recorded a contemporary saying "The Spaniard eats, the German drinks, and the English exceed in both." He was not the only one who disapproved of his countrywomen consuming sausage and ale in the taverns of the town.

The adventures of the East India Company increased the cheapness of oriental commodities. Sugar, dried fruit and spices were within the reach of all but the very poor. The fluctuation of harvests sent food prices wildly up and down. Various books of "Characters," a form in which the century excelled, contain many references to gluttony, drunkeness and feasting. Breton tells us how at Christmas "The Beasts, Fowle and Fish, come to a general execution . . . Stolne Venison is sweet, and a fat coney worth money." Overbury says of *A French Cook* : "he's such an enemy to beef and mutton. To conclude, he were only fit to make a funeral feast, where men should eat their victuals in mourning." During this time Mary Fairfax was busy adding recipes to the manuscript book begun in the previous century, which she had inherited from her mother. Some of her dishes sound delectable. Shoulder of mutton stuffed with oysters and hard boiled eggs, is one ; while her pancakes of eggs, cream and sherry, sound equally delicious. She used flowers : 'Violettes, Roses and Marigolds' for sweets and from clover blossoms made a pudding sauce.

Meanwhile the poor ate all that was cheap and plentiful. Gabriel Harvey lived to be more than eighty on a simple diet of buttered roots and sheep's trotters, since he had no money for better fare. It is he who tells us how Greene died, begging 'for a penny pot of Malmsey.' While Fletcher writes of feasting preparations :

> "The duck and the drake shall swim in a lake
> Of onions and claret below."

The Italians and French exerted considerable influence on the tables of the great. Massinger, whose father had seen service as steward to the noble Herbert family, describes in much detail the luxuries of the town ; how all the confectioners were 'ransacked to furnish out a banquet'—a repast served in another room after the meal proper. Sucking pigs—

Will's Best Coffee Powder at Manwarings Coffee House in Falcon Court over against St Dunstans Church in Fleet Street

AN ADVERTISEMENT FOR WILL'S COFFEE HOUSE c. 1700

'A fortnight fed with dates, and muskadine,' 'their thirty-pound buttered eggs,' 'pies of carp's tongues,' 'pheasants drenched with ambergris.' His "carcases of three fat wethers bruised for gravy, to make sauce for a single peacock" surely inspired Washington Irving; while Pepys had his 'botago,' a sausage made of eggs and mullet's blood, beaten up together. But not all is so fine; Flecknoe complains *Of an English Inn* : "... meat so tough and raw-roasted, as spite of teeth y'are forced to leave it to the house." In this century I find a first reference to the two course meal, in Earle's *Microcosmography*, where he records that the second course having gone up, the cook can retire to sleep. This practice was to remain in country districts at least for nearly two hundred years; for Horace Walpole, Parson Woodforde and Jane Austen speak of such meals being provided for the delectation of "company."

It was an odd age for, in the midst of all the lavish feeding and drinking, the struggle between Cavaliers and Roundheads was taking place. The Puritan influence did much to destroy the traditional splendour of English fare, as it was against the use of wine and spice. The struggle was a long one, for the habit of eating certain delicious food is not readily foregone. The Lord Protector's favourite dish, from the region of his native place, was roast veal with oranges. But it does seem to me that the steady deterioration of the English Table began with the coming of Puritanism. Anthony Wood complains of a dinner eaten at his brother's house: "Cold meat, cold entertainment, cold reception, cold clownish woman," which suggests that by 1673 hospitality had begun its fall from grace. Good things happened even so, for the English began, rather timidly, to discover that vegetables had other uses than in soups and salads. Misson, a visitor from France, tells us of boiled salt beef cooked with cabbage, carrots and turnips, with plenty of pepper and salt and 'swimming in Butter.' It was he who so delighted in the English Pudding and thought the inventor BLESSED. He describes Christmas Pie as a "most learned Mixture of Neat's-tongues, Chicken, Eggs, Sugar, Raisins, Lemon and Orange Peel, various Kinds of Spicery, etc.," which he maintains was "eaten everywhere." It is from the latter half of the century that genuine English cookery books seem to date. Gervase Markham wrote a whole series of volumes on a variety of subjects: including compilations on cookery and husbandry, which had considerable success; these may be said to have influenced English diet. Few of us to-day could eat a herring pie made according to his recipe, with its various ingredients of sugar and spice. Soon such books were pouring from the presses. The Countess of Kent, Lord Ruthven, Sir Theodore Mayerne and Sir Kenelm Digby (he warning his readers of the perils of tea drinking) all produced books of recipes, (it is only proper to state that many of these were unpleasant remedies for various ailments, however), which does suggest that an intelligent interest was taken in food and its preparation. During the government of Oliver Cromwell, Jos. Cooper, advertising himself as "chiefe Cooke to the late King," published *The Art of Cooking*. The Countess of Rutland's recipe for making 'The Rare Banbury Cake' was included in *The Compleat Cook*, while another offered a 'sallet of Rosebuds and Clove Gilly Flowers.' In 1656 Mounsier Marnette was paying compliments to English women, every one of whom "are so well versd in the Pastry Art." While Hannah Woolley wrote another cookery book: "to testifie to the scandalous World that I do not altogether spend my Time idlely." Spirit drinking was much fostered by the heavy taxes on beer and ale. By 1692

COVENT GARDEN MARKET IN THE EIGHTEENTH CENTURY
Oil painting by B. Nebot, fl. 1735-1760

the annual output of the licensed brewers of 2,088,000 barrels of beer, had fallen by 565,000. And after the prohibition of imported French brandy, the manufacture and consumption of English gin increased alarmingly.

By 1680 a vegetable market was established at Covent Garden. Culpepper mentions parsnips and carrots, while earlier, Parkinson gives artichokes, asparagus, endive, radishes, potatoes, spinach, peas, cucumbers, melons and pumpkins. Walpole, a century later, was to rejoice at the discovery of a print which showed Charles II accepting from his gardener the first pineapple ever grown in this country. The newly founded Royal Society gave a profound blessing to the humble potato, but it remained yet a rarity. Asparagus was sold fairly cheaply, while artichokes were expensive. In 1675 the Rev. Henry Teonge records in his diary, aboard ship on the coast of Africa, eating for dinner "a rump of beef, a little salted and well roasted," they had a couple of fat pullets to follow, drinking 'white ribiola.' Evelyn wrote of salads in his *Acetaria*, laying down certain principles, approved of by gastronomists of to-day, advocating a mixture of mustard, oil and vinegar for the dressing. The even more famous diarist Pepys describes many a meal made for the entertainment of his guests ; one of his special dinners included a fricasse (an Elizabethan term) "of rabbits, and chicken, a leg of mutton boiled, three carps in a dish, a great dish of a side of lamb, a dish of roasted pigeons, a dish of four lobsters, three tarts, a lamprey pie, a moast rare pie, a dish of anchoves, good wine of several sortes . . . most neatly dressed by our own only mayde." He makes many references to the coffee-house ; the first was opened in London

31

by a Turkish merchant in 1652. Some twenty years later a book was on sale, translated from French and Spanish, explaining the virtues of coffee, tea and chocolate, with the correct methods of making these new beverages ; not all of which achieved equally rapid success. Milton in his great poem, when he tells of the delicious meal prepared for Raphael in the garden of Eden, illustrates the excellence of his own taste ; in writing of Eve :

> ". . . on hospitable thoughts intent
> What choice to chuse for delicacie best,
> What order, so contriv'd as not to mix
> Tastes, not well joynd, inelegant, but bring
> Taste after taste upheld with kindliest change,"

and then,

> ". . . for drink the Grape
> She crushes, inoffensive moust, and meathes
> From many a berrie, and from sweet kernels prest
> She tempers dulcet creams . . ."

Other poets offer more substantial fare. While Butler in *Hudibras* mentions champagne, Herrick provides harvest celebrations :

> "Foundation of your feast, fat beef
> With upper stories, mutton, veal."

Brawn, pies, custards and 'all tempting frumenty' are all on the board. He cursed the host whose hospitality having promised much, provides only 'a ragd-soust-neats-foot with sick vinegar' and 'Beere small as Comfort, dead as Charity.'

The century that had seen so much novelty and change was drawing to a close. Tea, in spite of the heavy tax upon it, was being imported by the East India Company, but it was still too heavily taxed for all but the well-to-do, who drank it in the Chinese fashion, weak and without milk, paying rather more than twenty shillings a pound for the privilege.

A sign of the times was the notorious Calves' Head Club, which ate the head of the animal cooked in all sorts of ways in order to show their contempt for the executed monarch, so that it became the custom of republican politicians to dine off this dish on January 30th.

Jealousy of the privileged East India Company helped the Puritans in their campaign against spices and delicacies of the East, so that only the richer classes could afford such luxuries.

SMITHFIELD MEAT MARKET

Water colour by Thomas Rowlandson, c. 1816

A VICTORIAN PICNIC

Coloured engraving, c. 1860

VI

The way to Queen Anne's heart seems to have been through a good meal. She won the approval of no less an authority than Brillat-Savarin himself and seems to have employed an army of cooks and confectioners. In other periods bread formed the staple article of diet, but in this—meat was the mainstay of all able to afford it. The prodigal half-century can be gauged from numerous records. Swift tells Stella how he drank Burgundy and Tokay when out to dinner. The consumption of Port was vastly stimulated by the Methuen Treaty with Portugal to the disadvantage of the French. *The London Spy* gives malicious and lively pictures of the cheap eating houses and taverns. Gin drinking among the poor was a growing scandal, since they drank the wildest and most dangerous concoctions manufactured and sold by the unscrupulous.

A menu for a dinner party of the period suggests a dish of fish, removed later for a tureen of 'Soop,' a venison pasty, a chine of mutton, a 'White Fricassee,' beans and bacon, an orange pudding, tongue and 'Colliflowers.' The second course ordered partridges, 'Sweetmeat Tarts,' three young rabbits, 'Marrow Pasties,' roast pigeons, veal-sweetbreads and a dish of young peas.

Billingsgate quickly established itself as the great fish market. The hucksters sold oysters as cheaply as two shillings the hundred ; buyers could, if they so chose, purchase gilt gingerbreads from the next barrow. Among the cries of the town—'Lilly-white vinegar', 'Milk maids, below,' 'Buy my artichokes, mistress,' 'Ripe cowcumbers,' 'Ripe speragas,' 'Any baking pears' were but few of those which greeted the ears of the populace.

Martin Lister, physician to Queen Anne, printed an annotated edition of Aspicius' epicurean practices of the ancients, which excited attention and drew from Dr. William King a long poem *The Art of Cooking*, dedicated to Estcourt, the actor-founder of the first Beefsteak Club, in which he tells of 'Mac'rel' dressed with gooseberry sauce, and fennel for salmon, lobster and crab. Elaborate sweets were devised, the trifle made a first appearance as 'A Floating Island,' while Burned Creams and Sylabubs grew more and more fashionable now that women were taking to the writing of cookery books. Before the death of the gourmet Queen, Patrick Lamb, her cook, published *Royal Cookery*, and *The Queen's Royal Cookery* appeared with a portrait of Anne as a frontispiece, while her confectioner, Mary Eales, brought out her own recipes in 1718.

Lord Chesterfield thought that carving was a necessary part of every gentleman's equipment ; he employed a famous man cook, who tells in his compilation how a 'nourishing' broth could be made from a couple of hundred sparrows and other ingredients. Pope, in a letter to Swift, admits he "had nothing for Dinner but Mutton-broth, Beans and Bacon, and a Barn-door Fowl." His line from *The Dunciad*: "Thy truffles,

Perigord ! Thy hams, Bayonne !" proves the English connoisseur was well aware of foreign delicacies ; Addison wrote of the English brewers "They can squeeze Bordeaux out of the sloe, and draw Champagne from an apple." The art of faking made great strides, and the conditions in the town dairies were filthy. Defoe travelled about the country, then gave a charming account of the activities of the communal cheese makers of Cheddar : "without dispute, it is the best Chese that *England* affords, if not, that the whole World affords." At best, it fetched eightpence a pound, while the rival Cheshire commodity was sold for a mere twopence half-penny. The Englishman abroad, in spite of finding three courses against his native two, had a poor opinion of foreign tables. Horace Walpole wrote to a friend "the English can eat no meat, nor be civil to any God but their own." He also complained from Paris, "a third of the dishes is patched up with sallads, butter, puff-paste, or some such miscarriage of a dish." And this from a man of modest appetite, who swore he saw no difference between a Norfolk country gentleman and a sirloin: "Men who are mountains of roast beef." Had not Fielding sung "Oh ! The Roast beef of England, And old England's roast beef" which must have been roared by thousands during country feasts up and down the land. Among the fashionable foods of the century were the *oglio*, a highly spiced hash of meat and vegetables ; *salmugundi*, a salad of meat, fish, onions and herbs dressed with vinegar ; custards of all kinds ; some flavoured with spirits or sherry, earned grand names for themselves ; while the older, more simple flummery, made out of eggs or oatmeal, was still served; frumenty, an ancient dish of husked wheat boiled in milk to a thick porridge, sweetened with plums and sugar, was still eaten in country districts. Tea-drinking became more and more popular ; people learned that if they spread bread with butter, cutting it in thin slices, it made a delicious accompani-ment to the new drinks. The rich took to simple breakfasts of tea, coffee, or chocolate with hot rolls at eleven o'clock, making an excellent preparation for the heavy dinners and suppers ahead. Eating clubs became a rage and The Sublime Society of Beefsteaks attracted many famous and wealthy members, during its long existence of more than a hundred years. It was an age of conversation : among the instructions laid down for a successful dinner party one ruled that the number of guests should not be less than three nor more than seven. The coffee-houses attracted the wits and the beaux ; so that if a private individual wished for good company at his table he had to provide substantial attractions.

In 1747 *The Art of Cookery* appeared, which, while it did not actually give us "First catch your hare," started off a long chase, in which even the eminent joined, and some aver to this day that the quarry was never run down. The author (whoever he or she was) wrote "Take your hare when it is cased" : (skinned). As was often the way in those days, no name appeared on the title page ; the writer modestly concealing identity as

AN EIGHTEENTH CENTURY DINNER
Engraving by P. Bouché

A Lady. The book had immediate success. The third edition named Mrs. Glasse as the author. At a dinner party given by Dilly, the bookseller, Dr. Johnson, Boswell and Anna Seward were among the guests. Johnson held forth on cooking, saying that he could write a better book than any existent: "Then as you cannot make bad meat good, I would tell you what is the best butcher's meat, the best beef, the best pieces: how to choose young fowls; the proper seasons of different vegetables; and then how to roast and boil, and compound." Dilly countered by suggesting that Mrs. Glasse's *Cookery* was the best yet, and written by a Dr. Hill.

Johnson disagreed. The book, he argued, contained a mistake that a scientist would never have made. "You shall see" he promised, "what a book of cookery I shall make!" The poetess exclaimed "That would be Hercules with a distaff indeed." Apparently Dr. Johnson silenced the company with his rejoinder: "No, Madam. Women can spin very well, but they cannot make a good book of cookery." That was more than forty years later. If Johnson had no opinion of women as writers on the subject, he had nothing against them as cooks: blue stockings yet deserving the *cordon bleu* seem to have been to his taste. Madame D'Arblay tells a pleasing story of her first meeting with him at Streatham. Dr. Johnson, in the middle of dinner, asked Mrs. Piozzi (Thrale) what was in some little pies that were near him. "Mutton," answered she, "so I don't ask you to eat any, because I know you despise it." "No, madam, no," cried he, "I despise nothing that is good of its sort, but I am too proud now to eat of it." Mrs. Piozzi herself recalled "One day at dinner I meant to please Mr. Johnson particularly with a dish of very young green peas. 'Are they not charming?' said I to him, while he was eating them—'perhaps (said he) they would be so— to a *pig*.'" But he could and did appreciate good food. "It is a very great thing to dine with the Canons of Christ Church" was one remark; while on another occasion he praised with "Sir, we could not have had a better dinner, had there been a *Synod of Cooks*."

Many lively passages on eating and drinking are to be found in Amory's odd novel of the period, *The Life and Adventures of John Buncle Esq.* Smollet tells of adulterated bread and vile butter. Vinegar was adulterated; the increasingly popular pickles were made attractive by the addition of copper sulphate; various forms of sophistication were applied to wine, beer and spirits. Tea became so cheap that anyone who cared to might buy it. Travellers from the continent found a new excellence, for besides bread and butter, "thin as poppy-leaves," there was buttered toast!

Goldsmith's *The Haunch of Venison* can still charm us; another piece, less well known, shows how he likened his friends to various dishes with wit and skill. Often hard up, some of Goldsmith's accounts from his landlady (which have been preserved) reveal he paid a shilling a pint for Mountain, while ale was merely twopence: port at two shillings a bottle, while wine and cake cost eighteen pence.

A cookery school was opened in London by a man who offered to teach ladies the art privately in their own homes. He, too, had published a successful book on cooking. By the time the third George came to the throne, increasing population taxed food production; a series of bad harvests burdened the poor and conditions went from bad to worse. By contrast we have the picture of Miss Chudleigh giving a supper party for the Duke of Kingston. The meal was very fine, served in two rooms. Tokay was drunk: on all the sideboards and even on chairs there were "pyramids and troughs of strawberries and cherries": "You would have

Madam

The Honour of your Company is desired with ye Ladies & Gentlewomen Practitioners

In the

Art of Pastery and Cookery

SCHOLARS to Nath: Meystnor:

To dine at

on Thursday the
and bring

This ticket with you.

INVITATION TO ATTEND A COOKERY EXHIBITION
Engraving c. 1775

thought she was kept by Vertumnus." Buns and buttered muffins became the rage ; the Duchess of Northumberland declared in a contest at *bouts-rimés* that she preferred the latter to the finest *oglio*. Hannah More gives an account of "a very sober party" at a dinner given for "Madame la Chevalière D'Eon" who got rather too gay if allowed to consume a bottle or so of a favoured Burgundy.

To turn from the fashionable and known to the merely comfortable is to find astounding evidence of the pleasures of the table in the lives of the obscure. *The Diary of a Country Parson* gives a vivid picture of life in college and country. Norfolk, a county ever celebrated for good living, gave a superb one to James Woodforde who brewed his own beer ; did some black marketing in the shape of smuggled brandy, rum and gin ; bottled his own wine ; coursed the hare with his own greyhounds ; kept his own cows and pigs, and who could also cook a meal for himself if he chose. He was hospitable, and so was his niece who kept house for him. I have only room here for one of the elaborate dinners with which they delighted to entertain : nine people sat down to table and ate "six pair of fryed Soal, a very fine Leg of Mutton rosted, boiled Ham and three Chicken, Beans, a boiled plumb Pudding, and new Potatoes. 2nd Course a Couple of rost Ducks and Peas. Berries Charter (old English fruit fool?) Rasberry Cream, red Currant and Gooseberry Tarts and black Currant Tartlets. Dessert, french Olives, Raspberries, Cherries, three sorts of Strawberries and White Currants, Mountain, and Port Wines." Woodforde's bread bill can never have caused him any anxiety for his household of seven consumed less than two pounds of flour a person in a week ! Capacity may be gauged from niece Nancy who ate for dinner one day, some rather fat salt boiled beef, "a good deal of a nice rost duck, and plenty of boiled Damson Pudding." Her dessert consisted of "green-gage Plumbs, some Figgs, and Rasberries and Cream." On that occasion she did overdo things rather, but was well enough by dinner time next day for "rost Neck of Mutton."

Carl Moritz, the German pastor, thought poorly of the average Englishman's midday meal, of "half-boiled or half-roasted meat," ". . . Cabbage-leaves, boiled in plain water . . . a sauce made of flour and butter, the usual method of dressing vegetables." He complained too about our coffee, which he described (he might have been writing yesterday) as a prodigious quantity of brown water !

Sir Frederick Eden's monumental *The State of the Poor*, told of the scarcity of milk ; the labourers' diet was usually "bread, butter, cheese, pickled pork, and a little butcher's meat." He was shocked by their fondness for highly sweetened tea, which he found they drank three times daily. He thought since they could not afford beer, they ought to spend their tea money on barley for broth. And Arthur Young, who studied them with equal care, was not more sympathetic.

THE KITCHEN AT THE REFORM CLUB
Engraving by W. Radcliffe after G. B. Moore from *London Interiors*

VII

The new century brought many changes into the lives of the English ;
though for most of them it started off badly enough, with the prices of
staple foods rising steadily. The plight of the poor was desperate ; village
life was in decay, owing to the loss of ancient privileges, resulting from the
steady encroachment of the various Enclosure Acts. Deserting the hamlets
they moved to the hungry towns, where conditions rapidly worsened
under their influx. Cobbett gives many details of the wretchedness of
the labouring classes noted in various parts of the country. The inns,
once so prosperous, began their decline. Travellers complained that many
of them were filthy ; while their fare, poor in quality, was expensive in
price. Even country hospitality seemed in disrepute, while war clouds
gathered and grumbled.

In London the wealthy went on much as usual, and since the Prince
Regent was a gourmet, he, no doubt, helped to maintain their standards.
It was at his suggestion that Watiers, a dining club noted for its luxurious
cooking, was founded. Captain Gronow, one of the Regent's set, describes

the glory of Crockford's where "a supper of the most exquisite kind" was served to the members without payment. To dine out was an expectation fulfilled for "as darkness after day" after turtle and Mulligatawny soup came salmon, turbot and smelts ; with saddle of mutton, a baron of beef, fowls, ham and tongue as the second course. Potatoes were served, plain and boiled with everything but the sweet, other vegetables were often served cold, but never with a sauce.

In spite of Charles Lamb's passion for pork, so ardently stressed in a letter to Coleridge, most of the literary men's taste seems to have been for "a large cold bottle and a small hot bird." Who can forget Hazlitt's descriptions of reading, while he ate chicken or pheasant, and drank sherry or coffee? He was knowledgeable about food and inns. But here we must thrust through the galaxy, (leaving Keats to enjoy his Claret; and Byron, with his complaint of the ladies, who "always had the wings of the chicken") since Thomas Love Peacock towers over them all on the subject. Not only did he write poems about food, but his novels are stuffed with meals ; the people who eat them have much to say on the subject of delicious wines and foods. No other English novelist has ever written so well or so much for the gourmet as he. At much the same time another English eccentric was preoccupied by the various problems of the table. Dr. William Kitchiner not only learned to cook for himself, but wrote learnedly for the benefit of others ; producing his famous *Cook's Oracle*, which is the forerunner of the cookery book of our own times with its precise directions as to quantities and method. Creevey has many amusing glimpses of the great at table ; nor does he hesitate to blame the careless : at one house the dinner "was damnable in cookery, comfort and everything else" while at another "no roast beef on the side-table but only a sucking pig," a third gave him "excellent and plentiful dinners . . . a table with a barrel of oysters and hot pheasant, etc., wheeled into the drawing room every night half-past-ten."

In 1827 London prices included "Chickens are 15/- a couple . . . cock's combs 22/- a pound, and it takes a pound and a half to make a dish." Lord Cowper tells how William IV "ate very heartily of turtle, accompanying it with punch, sherry, and champagne." Dinner always lasted a long time : "the king must have drunk a couple of bottles of claret before we left the table." A dinner at a fashionable club cost not less than 'a *pund*.'

Thomas Walker published his *Art of Dining* in 1835. One of his dinners for eight people consisted of turtle soup with punch to drink, his guests were next given whitebait and champagne, then grouse and claret. The sweet was of apple fritters served with jelly. Thackeray's passion for whitebait of the Greenwich variety led him to write : "It has an almost angelic delicacy of flavour : it is as fresh as the recollections of childhood—it wants a Corregio's pencil to describe it with sufficient

40